A Brief History of
Hawaii

by George Armitage

Published and distributed by The Islander Group
Copyright by George Armitage

Tiki God of Kukailimoku

*Dedicated
to my wife whose
earnest, able research has
helped so much in all my work.*

LONG BEFORE PEARL HARBOR

Hawaii's Historical Highlights

This thumbnail sketch is an attempt to streamline Hawaii's history into some 8000 words. Few names or dates will be used, and mental excursions down tempting historical byways will be largely avoided. Some may adversely criticize this rash attempt but at least none shall say it isn't brief. Thus, in the hope that it will help interested newcomers in these stirring times to understand just a little about the background on the 50th State, Hawaii,* here, for the busy person's benefit, is abbreviation with a vengeance.

*Congress approved Statehood for Hawaii, March 12, 1959.

EARLY-DAY
VIEW OF
NUUANU
PALI

CHAPTER I

TOPS OF MIGHTY MOUNTAINS

LIKE many islands of the Pacific the Hawaiian Islands are volcanic in origin. Some writers say, that like the lost Atlantis, there was once a vast continent in the South Pacific which was submerged during a cataclysmic disaster, and only the highest mountain peaks were left above the sea. But geologists are agreed that these island peaks have been built by slow outpourings of lava flows.

On Hawaii island the oft snow-capped summits of Mauna Kea and Mauna Loa rear their hoary heads nearly 14,000 feet into the sky, constituting the highest mountain masses on the earth, with an elevation of 31,750 feet direct from the ocean floor around them.

These islands, however, are still in the process of formation. On the Big Island, volcanic action is in evidence everywhere, especially in Hawaii National Park. Because these islands were formed through the eons by molten lava gushing up from a rift under the sea, there are few commercial minerals in Hawaii and no coal or oil. Perhaps that is why the natives had not advanced beyond the stone age when these islands were discovered. So much for her geology.

People who are interested in Hawaii's tumultuous past also ask, "Where did the Hawaiians come from?" The answers are long and varied, but for all practical purposes this one will suffice: The only place where Hawaii's lovely *lei* custom (giving of floral garlands) still survives (outside the South Seas), is India. Why? Because in the dim past Hawaii's progenitors came out of Southern Asia and eventually migrated to the East Indies. Hawaiian place names like Oahu are still found there. Even the name Hawaii may have been *Jawa-i'i* (Little Java). Though scientists still argue about the exact routes of these migrations, they generally agree that the direction was eastward through the hundreds of islands that make up Pacific Oceania.

Some scientists who have thoroughly studied the subject say the early Hawaiians' place of departure for their voyage to their present home was a little island called *Havaii*, near Tahiti, in the Society Group (French). In those days there must have been a good many comings and goings between Hawaii and Tahiti, even though the islands were more than 2,000 miles apart, because the channel between Lanai and Kahoolawe even today bears the revealing name, Kealaikahiki, or "The Way to Tahiti." Kealaikahiki Channel, between Lanai and Kahoolawe in Hawaii, was where the voyagers lined up their big outrigger canoes for the return voyage and set their courses by the stars.

These earlier peoples in Tahiti also apparently jumped in several other directions besides towards Hawaii, for today the Maoris in New Zealand, the Samoans, Tongans, Easter Islanders, and others in so-called Polynesia (many islands) all resemble each other physically and have similar languages and customs.

Others will tell you that the first Hawaiians came from the East—or the West; that the Islands were discovered by, and named after, a great pre-historic navigator called Hawaiiloa; but don't let this bother you. Polynesians had no written language until the coming of the missionaries, and word of mouth accounts handed down for countless generations are so allegorical that it is difficult to determine where fancy stops and fact begins.

Probably there is some truth in *all* the theories of Hawaii's origin. Certainly the Polynesians were wonderful and curious-minded seamen, traversing thousands of unknown ocean miles in great double outrigger canoes, with no navigating facilities except the wind, stars, and ocean currents to guide them, and with no provision for cold storage rations. Instead, the Hawaiians planted sea-going farms on the wide platforms which joined the canoes, and raised gardens of taro and sweet potatoes. These "farms" also maintained live pigs and chickens for the long journey and in the deep hulls of the canoes were stored seed coconuts and plant cuttings with which to develop the new islands of Hawaii upon which they eventually settled.

CHAPTER II

CAPTAIN COOK STARTED IT

AN English explorer, Captain James Cook, who for some years had been prowling around the Pacific uncovering many new islands, actually started recorded Hawaiian history when he accidentally came upon the islands on a trip north from Tahiti.

Some students of history are inclined to believe that Captain Cook wasn't the first to discover Hawaii, for they suspect that he had previous knowledge of its existence from certain charts made by earlier Spanish navigators. Islands which corresponded with the approximate position of Hawaii were clearly indicated on these charts. Then, too, many Hawaiian customs and legends suggest previous visits by outsiders, including the Dutch as well as the Spanish.

It was in 1778 that Captain Cook sailed up to Waimea on Kauai island, just at the time when George Washington and our tattered little Continental army in revolution against Captain Cook's mother country, were shivering at Valley Forge. And if it hadn't been for the open-mindedness of our Yankee ancestors, the news of that famous discovery might have come via America.

This is the story: Benjamin Franklin, America's eminent minister in France, ordered his rugged American compatriots on the high seas, if they ran into Captain Cook's ship, to allow it to proceed home to England unmolested.

Furthermore, while Captain Cook must be given full credit for his discovery, it is altogether possible that an American might have been first to lay eyes on Hawaii's verdant mountains set in sapphire seas. For, strangely enough, on Captain Cook's own ship, the Resolution, there were two Americans, one from New England, and another from Virginia, and either, if awake and looking in the right direction, might have seen us first.

THE KING
EXTENDS
A WARM
ALOHA

CHAPTER III

STRONG MEN WITH LONG NAMES

WHEN Captain Cook first met the Hawaiians he found that some of their kings and chiefs were strong men with long names and warlike tendencies. The King of Hawaii Island at that time was Kalaniopuu, and struggling for supremacy, even then, was his bright young nephew, Kamehameha. Kamehameha's birthplace is given as Kohala, Hawaii, but the exact date and place are debatable. His father was believed to have been Chief Keoua, half brother of King Kalaniopuu, but some have claimed that Kamehameha was a son of Kahekili, the fighting King of Maui. There was a Kamehameha-nui (Big Kamehameha) on that island who was a brother of Kahekili, but any study of Hawaiian genealogy gets very involved. Certainly Kamehameha, whatever his antecedents, was the wonderman of his day—strong, fearless and wise, withal a pagan.

During all his conquests of Hawaiian territory, Kamehameha took time out to combine heart interests with war-like efforts. Often upon defeating an adversary he wooed and won important high born women in the enemy camp, and by taking them to wife, not only added ability and charm to his court, but also cemented relations with the conquered instead of widening the breach.

Like Columbus' arrival in the Americas, Captain Cook's coming, (definitely recorded as the first arrival from the outside world), created a tremendous stir in the Islands. Never before had the Hawaiians seen real ships, and they believed Cook's vessels were floating islands, the masts and spars resembling trees. Hence, today the Hawaiian word for both ship and island is the same, i.e., *moku*. Also because their word-of-mouth *mele* (they had no writing then), prophesied that someday the Polynesian god, Lono, might come back that way, they thought Cook was Lono and so termed and treated him.

The famous Captain was probably too busy to bother his head over a native superstition. Nevertheless some historians have criticized Cook, declaring he purposely allowed the simple natives to worship him as a diety, because in their eyes he appeared a superman. Indeed, the explorer and his men seemed able to perform miracles, such as belching forth sparks from their mouths (smoking), and sticking their hands right into their bodies (pockets)! And didn't they carry long sticks of iron (muskets) which hurled a death more violent than the fiery blasts of Pele?

The native Hawaiians went wild over English possessions, especially anything made of iron which was almost non-existent in Hawaii. Barter for cutting weapons was particularly brisk and, ironically enough, Cook was killed by one of his own trade knives.

During his protracted stay on Hawaii Island, Captain Cook had been royally treated by the natives, and relations with them were friendly, at least on the surface. But whether he knew it or not, when he finally sailed away and headed home to England the Hawaiians' aloha was wearing out. But, caught in a storm off north Hawaii which broke a mast, Captain Cook, unluckily, was forced to return to Kealakekua Bay, and he never left it again!

The Hawaiians cherish an old superstition that it is bad luck to return after starting a journey. It surely was bad for Captain Cook, for when he sailed back into Kealakekua Bay, to his surprise he found that atmosphere strained and unfriendly. The truth was that the natives had grown weary of continually provisioning Captain Cook and his crew. In short, Captain Cook, like a tarrying week-end guest, had worn out his welcome and the *aloha* committee had quit. Unknown to the Englishmen their popularity was on the wane, and it took only a stolen British row boat to start a row.

In the *melee* which followed, Captain Cook, who was believed to be a god, was wounded the same as any ordinary native. When the Hawaiians realized that Cook was no immortal, they felt grossly deceived and killed him. The shapely shaft of a monument on Kealakekua Bay, Hawaii, marks the spot where he and some of his comrades died. The soil on which it stands belongs appropriately to Cook's mother country as it was given to Great Britain by A. S. Cleghorn and his wife, Princess Likelike (sister of King Kalakaua and Queen Liliuokalani).

Actually it is said that the deed for this property is held by an old Honolulu family which donates to Great Britain the land for the monument to its distinguished son.

CHAPTER IV

KAMEHAMEHA TAKES ALL

IN Captain Cook's day each main island of the Hawaiian group—Kauai, Oahu, Maui, and Hawaii—was a jealous independent kingdom with separate monarchs eternally trying to subjugate his neighbor next door. Kamehameha the First grew up and was nurtured in this warring atmosphere. When his uncle, King Kalaniopuu died, Kamehameha quickly forestalled several other ambitious chiefs by capturing Hawaii island for himself.

Benefitting from the brilliant fighting and sage advice of John Young and Isaac Davis, two British seamen whom Kamehameha, the Great had made members of his cabinet, this ambitious and able young warrior started a campaign to master all the islands. Along with other information of vital importance, Young and Davis taught Kamehameha the use of the cannon, musket, and gunpowder, modern weapons which proved decisive factors in ultimate victory for Kamehameha.

One of the first cannon balls fired in the battle of Nuuanu Valley killed Kaiana, a handsome Kauai chief and Kamehameha's most formidable adversary. For many years Chief Kaiana had been Kamehameha's close friend and advisor, but quarrels over Kaahumanu, Kamehameha's favorite queen, and a feeling of jealousy over Chief Kaiana's ability and leadership, sowed seeds of distrust.

It was on the island of Molokai, while en route to the critical battle of Oahu, that Kaiana decided, after Kamehameha had called an important council of war and left him out, that his number was up. Taking part of Kamehameha's army with him, Kaiana stole away and joined forces with King Kalanikupule on Oahu. When Kaiana's wife learned that her husband was deserting she refused to leave with him, but elected instead to stay with Kamehameha. To Chief Kaiana it must have seemed like the irony of fate that his own wife should desert him for the King when much of the original quarrel had arisen over Kamehameha's fear that his favorite Queen, Kaahumanu, was partial to Kaiana.

On Oahu, Kaiana brought his army up from the windward side of Nuuanu Pali and joined forces with King Kalanikupule entrenched in Nuuanu valley above Honolulu. There they met Kamehameha's horde but from the first, the Oahuans were on the losing side, and many of their men were driven up the valley and hurled over the Pali. The rout really began when one of the first blasts from Kamehameha's cannon cut Chief Kaiana in two. And that was the last of the colorful and intrepid Hawaiian warrior who finally found himself on the wrong side of the fence. Oahu was conquered, Kamehameha became supreme ruler of the entire Hawaiian group, and forever afterwards, as monarchy, republic, and territory, the Islands would be as one.

The Island of Kauai was never actually captured by Kamehameha the First, but later an army of his son, Kamehameha II, did subdue revolting Kauaians. It was also during the reign of Kamehameha II that King Kaumualii of Kauai was abducted and thereafter lived in Honolulu, practically as a royal prisoner of the reigning family with which he more closely associated himself by marrying the late Kamehameha's favorite Queen, Kaahumanu. And never one for half-way measures, Kaahumanu responded by wedding on the same day the Kauai King's son!

By such an act it would seem as if royal women in Hawaii were scarce, but actually there was no rationing even of queens in those days. A king could have as many wives as he could manage, or support. Queen Kaahumanu never gave the conqueror a child but two of his wives were mothers or grandmothers of four Kamehameha kings who followed him.

FOR AGES
WOMEN
ENDURED
THE KAPU

CHAPTER V

THE WOMEN GET A BREAK

KAMEHAMEHA'S principal contribution to the Islands was in unifying them and ending forever the inter-island fighting. With the amazing outside world about which the Hawaiians had for so long been blissfully ignorant, he engineered first contacts and fostered commerce, and rather successfully, too, for a king whose country had enjoyed no earlier associations. But his son, Liholiho, who, upon his father's death became Kamehameha the Second, immediately found a more spectacular way of getting into the royal limelight. Liholiho abolished the pagan religion and every ridiculous taboo (*kapu*) which for centuries had been perpetuated on the fair sex, be their station high or low.

From infancy Liholiho was smart enough to notice that visiting sea captains and other *malihini* (newcomers) paid scant heed to taboo and apparently suffered no displeasure from the gods. Furthermore, the King knew that the Hawaiian religion had many drawbacks. The countless temples were expensive to build and maintain, and the priests were prone to assume too much power over the *alii* (royalty) as well as the laymen.

When his father died Liholiho took matters into his own hands; with one regal blow he swept away most of the *heiau* (temples), destroyed the hideous images of wood and stone, and declared that from then on the old gods were *pau* (through). Now, this wasn't done without some opposition. One chief of the old order on the island of Hawaii amassed a substantial force to defy Liholiho, but was decisively defeated. The old religion was destroyed, (outwardly at least), and from that time on the common people no longer had to fear the sacrificial altar.

As an advocate of women's rights in Hawaii, one of Liholiho's first constructive acts was to permit "co-educational" eating, which previously had been considered a high crime punishable by death. To give the new way vogue, one day he sat down to supper with his *wahine*, and lo, and behold! the heavens didn't fall, nor the diners drop dead. The king soon followed up with another edict that allowed women to eat such forbidden delicacies as bananas. In fact, he won the heart of every woman in the Islands as he freed them step by step.

That the women of his household, particularly his father's long suffering and widowed queens, put pressure on Liholiho to make these drastic changes should not detract one whit from his credit. It took intestinal fortitude even for a king to defy and toss out the window religious concepts that had been feared and practiced for centuries.

Later, after sanctity of the temples had been denied and most of the gods demolished, Princess Kapiolani, who had fallen under missionary influence, decided something should be done about the evil power of Pele, the awful fire-goddess of Hawaii's living volcano, who for centuries had instilled terror in the hearts of the Hawaiian people.

Today the journey to Kilauea crater is made over smooth paved highways, but then it was an arduous, painful trek along a dim trail, across rough lava flows, and through dense forests. But the indomitable princess, with a little band of faithful followers, made it in spite of obstacles, and at last stood on the brink of the terrifying fire-pit.

The Hawaiians opened their hymn books and lifted their voices to Jehovah, while Kapiolani with sure but trembling fingers, flung a handful of sacred *ohelo* berries right into Pele's face—that is, into the fire-pit itself. And nothing happened! Pele didn't lift an eyebrow.

It was proof enough for anyone that the Lord on high was far more powerful than the fire-goddess in her hell-like depths of Halemaumau. The stirring act was immortalized in verse by Lord Alfred Tennyson who was aware that it took a staunch heart to defy awful traditions of a dark and benighted past. But all this is a little ahead of the story to follow.

THE LOVELY
LEI CUSTOM
SURVIVES

CHAPTER VI

PACIFIC PILGRIMS BRING THE LIGHT

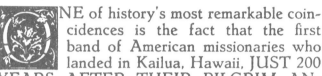 NE of history's most remarkable coin-cidences is the fact that the first band of American missionaries who landed in Kailua, Hawaii, JUST 200 YEARS AFTER THEIR PILGRIM AN-CESTORS HAD STEPPED ASHORE ON PLYMOUTH ROCK, found the Hawaiian stage already set for what they had come to do. Having repudiated their gods only the year before, the Hawaiians were ripe for the new and more gracious Lord whom they very rapidly accepted and never forsook. The missionaries introduced a new way of life in many ways besides the religious. They brought reading, writing, and 'rithmetic; carpentry and masonry; farming and trading. They promoted home life, love of family and good government.

People who are not students of Hawaiian his-tory are sometimes quick to criticize the mission-aries. Actually a Hawaiian first invited the missionaries to take up residence in the Islands. Opukahaia, a young native who went to New England on a sailing vessel, had begged Americans to visit his Islands and bring his people the enlightenment and benefits of Christianity. And, when the missionaries finally arrived, they found the Hawaiians living just as Opukahaia had described, in a wretched state, the common people oppressed, irresolute, and poverty stricken.

The Hawaiian people proved remarkably receptive to the new order. When one realizes that about 200 years ago they were living in the stone age, it is astounding how quickly the young and old, king and commoner alike, took to modern civilization. Hawaiian leaders readily accepted Christianity and promoted it amongst their followers. Of course all the *haole* people who came weren't missionaries or puritans. Many were the very opposite, and it was natural that the Hawaiians learned some bad with the good, like a taste for strong liquor and plug cut. Rip-roarin' seamen off the whaling ships fought the man-of-God for the native's interests, but in the end the churchmen triumphed, crime decreased, and industry and husbandry flourished.

AMERICAN
PRESENTED
FIRST HORSE

CHAPTER VII

SAILORS ON HORSEBACK

FTER Capt. Cook, the Islanders lived in a dream world, awaking each day to something brand new. The first cattle were landed in 1793 (one of the few dates we'll use and easy to remember because it was 300 years, and one, after Columbus discovered America). The cattle, presented by Lord Vancouver and put under a taboo, multiplied into what are Hawaii's big herds on present-day ranches and ranges. The famed Parker Ranch, one of the largest in the U.S.A., is still in the hands of a descendant of the original owner. Much of Hawaii's meat comes from this ranch and other big cattle ranches on several of the main islands.

Ten years later Richard Cleveland, an American ship captain, (the sea captains were always bringing things, even including mosquitoes), presented Kamehameha with horses, and detailed two sailors to show the King how they could be ridden. In the beginning the King wasn't so sure the steeds were worth their keep. But the more rapid means of transportation instantly appealed to the Hawaiians, and Spanish cowhands were imported from Mexico to teach the natives horsemanship and ranching. These cowboys were known as *Espagnola* (Spaniard), a term which gradually changed into the Hawaiian word *paniolo* (cowboy).

Today the cheery hard-riding Hawaiian *paniola* is as picturesque as his fore-runner, the Spaniard. He is a gay fellow, too, bedecking himself and his hat with a *lei* of fragrant *maile* vine and fern, and plunking a guitar or *ukulele* like a cavalier after he rides the ranges. Second to none as a roper of the wild cattle which roam his native mountains, he has bested his Mainland cowboy brothers in riding and roping contests at Mainland rodeos.

The ranchers on Hawaii go in largely for pure-bred cattle of the white-faced Hereford variety. Their pastures are scientifically planted with the best grasses. The ranch-houses and layouts are models of comfort, hospitality and efficiency, and the Hawaiian cowboys who ride the high meadows are as happy in that environment as they were down by their first love, the sea.

Later, when Hawaii became a popular shipping rendezvous, the Hawaiians showed as great an adaptability for sailing before the mast as riding the range. They became such desirable seamen that every ship's captain was finally obliged to post a $100 bond against each man's return. If some such a penalty hadn't been exacted, the Islands would soon have become a manless Eden.

HAWAIIANS
FIND TIME
FOR PLAY

CHAPTER VIII

EARLY TARS TOOK TOWN APART

HE first two Kamehamehas—Father and Son—started big business in Hawaii by selling out the Islands' sandalwood to English and Yankee fur traders, who took the popular scented wood to China for quick profit. But later and for fifty years, Hawaii's extra pocket money, a forerunner of the present century's lucrative and growing tourist trade, came from the hundreds of whaling ships that each winter sought sanctuary, supplies, and near tropic comforts in Hawaii. At times these ships were so thick in Honolulu's harbor that they were moored solidly together, and a person could walk from deck to deck across the harbor as on a wooden sidewalk. And if any faint hearts think today's sailors are sometimes on the free and easy side, they should have seen early-day before-the-masters in action. Those lusty Jack Tars took over the town and tore it at least partially apart, while the residents of Honolulu hied themselves indoors and pulled their storm windows in after them.

Speaking of tourists, who during the present century have flocked to Hawaii in great ocean liners and clippers, the first royal tourist to journey away from Hawaii was Chief Kaiana, already mentioned as the handsome ambitious brother of a King of Kauai. Kaiana, who later deserted the army of Kamehameha the First, went to China and returned. The next royal traveler was King Liholiho, Kamehameha the Second, who would see London, but died there of measles. Another Hawaiian monarch who died abroad (in San Francisco, in 1891) was the last king, Kalakaua.

A second son of the first Kamehameha was called Kamehameha the Third, but he might well have been termed "First" himself because of the many "firsts" chalked up during his reign. The new Hawaii was just beginning to click under Kamehameha the Third who was the most illustrious and longest ruling of the Kamehameha line. Excepting his father, he accomplished more for the Sandwich Islands than all the rest of the rulers put together. Incidentally, Hawaii was long known as the Sandwich Islands after the Earl of Sandwich who was Lord of the Admiralty in England when Captain Cook found the Islands. It was the same Sandwich who invented and named that modern-day luncheon delight.

Kamehameha the Third reigned from 1825-1854, and here is his box score of imposing "Firsts"; First laws published; Declaration of Rights adopted; first legislature convened; Royal School opened; first constitution proclaimed; first ambassadors sent to Europe; Punahou School started; first recognition of Hawaii's independence by the United States (also by Great Britain and France); restoration of independence by England; and because of this the King in gratitude coined the phrase which has ever since been the motto of Hawaii, *"Ua mau ke ea o ka aina i ka pono,"* (The life of the land is preserved in righteousness); first division of lands, (The Great Mahele in 1848), giving common people title to their property; protectorate offered U.S., annexation suggested, and a duty free treaty prepared (and not a c c e p t e d) ; first steamer arrived. A long reign and not always a merry one.

KALAKAUA
BUILT HIS
OWN PALACE

CHAPTER IX

UNCLE SAM KEEPS THE PEACE

THE two brothers, Kamehameha the Fourth and Fifth who followed on the throne, were nephews of the Second and Third Kamehamehas, and grandsons of the First. They were not outstanding. Their times saw the wane of the whaling trade and the beginning of what was destined to become Hawaii's far bigger business—sugar, and pineapple, the latter in the twentieth century rivalling sugar, much to the surprise of some old-time sugar men.

One of the first sugar ventures was on the island of Kauai when three young men from New England leased 980 acres of land and began planting. Although these young men and others who followed failed in their first attempts at sugar raising, by the time of America's Civil War, sugar was definitely established as the Islands' most important industry.

Out of the sugar business came the birth of big business which in turn developed and modernized the Islands. Today sugar represents an investment of many millions with profits shared by nearly 20,000 stockholders. Sugar plus pineapple means Hawaii. Hawaii has the ideal climate for both crops, each thriving at different levels and one a perfect complement to the other. Hawaii has also developed the latest scientific methods in producing them. Though sugar is a world commodity and the demand remains relatively constant, Hawaii's sugar crop represents but a small percentage of the world's supply, while her canned pineapple constitutes at least 75% of the earth's annual crop.

The rapid development of these two agricultural giants, and the failure of many others like cotton, sisal, silk, rubber, and tobacco, have been the glow and wane of the forge that has tempered and fused Hawaii. The many different peoples, mostly from the Orient, that have been needed in the development and maintenance of these industries, have come to Hawaii during the past century, and have become welded into the modern American way of life. So peacefully and harmoniously has this welding taken place that the State is well termed when it is called the "melting pot."

During her swaddling-clothes days, Little Red Riding Hood Hawaii was constantly menaced by some Big Bad Wolf old-world power. England had her three times—by discovery, by cession, and by force—but always gave her back. France almost took her over once; Russia made a pass or two at the lovely little lady but left nothing to show for it but Fort Street in Honolulu and two Russian Forts on Kauai, one at Hanalei and another star-shaped affair still visible at Waimea. Even Japan threatened the tiny Hawaii and extracted an indemnity. But Uncle Sam, ultimately to take the prodigy under his wing, was always comfortably in the offing, keeping the peace and demanding fair play for his struggling little friend way out there alone in the Pacific.

A LUAU—
RELIC OF
OLDEN DAYS

CHAPTER X

CAME THE MERRY MONARCH

UNALILO was the next king after Kamehameha the Fifth. Although distantly related to the Kamehamehas, he won his throne by popular election, and ruled just long enough—a little over a year —to quell one incipient mutiny. And because he thought his mother had been slighted Lunalilo decreed that he be buried all alone in the little *"Lunalilo Ka Moi"* (Lunalilo the King) tomb by the old Kawaiahao Hawaiian church on King Street. Then came the Merry Monarch, the last King of Hawaii, Kalakaua.

Kalakaua had visions of grandeur and a yen to be King in his own right. But times had changed and when he found that he could only be a constitutional monarch, he set out to have a good time, and let the boys in the other room— the counting room—do the worrying. He went off to the Mainland, had a grand reception in Washington, D.C., engineered the reciprocity treaty which got Uncle Sam's famed Pearl Harbor started, and really put Hawaiian sugar—now free of duty—on its feet. Kalakaua took a trip around the world, came back and built himself a palace, the present capitol building (and the only throne room in the United States), bought a regal jewel-studded crown—set it on his own head, and struck off numerous ribbons and orders for his friends. He went riding on the new Oahu Railroad that was rolling the milled sugar to the docks for refining in California, and even started his own "King's Navee," one ship, which made a single trip to Samoa and *pau* (finished).

He had a grand time and his last words—when he died in 1891 in San Francisco—were scratchily recorded on a new fangled doo-dad called a phonograph.

Unlike her brother, Queen Liliuokalani who followed him couldn't read the constitutional handwriting on the wall. She tried almost immediately to revert to the good old feudal days when a queen had only to cry, "Out with you!" and out you went forthwith. The Islands under American leadership had grown too modern, too strong, and too important to the peace and security of the United States and the Pacific for that sort of *opera bouffe* rule and the Queen not only lost her palace but was locked up in it. She was withal a gracious sovereign who in retirement forgave her deposers and lived happily to a ripe old age, always the beloved Queen.

The Queen's many talents included a mastery of music, and in the end she will probably be longer and better remembered by the world for her internationally sung "Aloha Oe" (Farewell to Thee) which, by the way, was written as much as a love song as a famous farewell.

CHAPTER XI

AMERICA'S WESTERN GATE

AFTER Queen Liliuokalani was eased out, and while the United States was trying to decide whether or not to accept these strutting Islands as a State, the queenless country tried a short term as a Republic with Hon. Sanford B. Dole as first and only president. With their strategic value greatly enhanced by the Spanish American war, Uncle Sam finally accepted the Islands as a Territory, (Hawaii had hoped to join the Union as a State), and the long flirtation between big, bluff, benign America and tiny, tempting Hawaii was over. A legislature elected by the people was established, President Dole became the first governor appointed by the President of the United States.

The marriage of Hawaii and America has been a grand success, and the two republics have lived happily and profitably together. There have been the usual family tiffs, and little

Hawaii used to think that Uncle Sam treated her more as an orphan than a spouse, but nowadays the Territory usually gets her due.* And why not? She is bigger than some states (Connecticut, Rhode Island, Delaware); more populous than others (Nevada, Wyoming, Delaware and Vermont); she pays more federal income than many individual states; and her cultural growth and military importance take a back seat to none of them. America knows now, since Pearl Harbor, that at Hawaii, Uncle Sam's military might truly guards—and—holds her Western Gate.

Hawaii is about 300 miles long (the main chain of eight inhabited islands), almost 14,000 feet high; nearly a million strong. (1983)

*Congress approved Statehood for Hawaii, March 12, 1959.

UNION STREET
WHEN CITY
WAS YOUNG

CHAPTER XII

FOUR "KINGS" DON'T ALWAYS WIN

BACK in the early days of high finance, Claus Spreckels, Island sugar broker and banker baron, thought he held Hawaii and King Kalakaua in the hollow of his hand. The usual story of a big poker game in which Kalakaua and he were the principal contestants has it that Kalakaua claimed a large pot with four kings, showing three and naming himself as the fourth. But other accounts have it that Spreckels made the kingly claim, naming himself as the fourth, (uncrowned, of course). Kalakaua, the real king, never forgave his pseudo and high-sounding friend for that irreverent boast, and the sugar baron was gradually squeezed out. Hawaii and hospitality are synonymous, but "you can't crowd a friend too far."

Hawaii has not only developed financial value, but she has created a culture for herself that any section of Mainland America might

ONLY THRONE
ROOM IN THE
UNITED STATES

well envy. Artists flock to Honolulu to paint the brilliant flowers and blue and purple seas, writers sing her praises and build their homes along the shores and beaches. Scientists come from afar to study her agricultural methods. Students of the South Seas, Asia, and the West have built an Institute of Pacific Relations at the University of Hawaii. In Hawaii merges the culture of the East and West but her hundred thousand school children troop to the public schools to study Americanism.

Hawaii is as modern as they come, with electric ice boxes, air conditioning, trolley buses, automatic phones, daily newspapers, movies, night clubs, lodges, churches; Hawaii is a good place to live—a good place to spend a vacation or indulge in an avocation.

Island people are a friendly, congenial sort with a natural workable philosophy. They know from experience that the different races can get along; that in a busy life there is still room for recreation and play—a *hula* and a song, polo and fishing, surfing and golf, even a symphony orchestra, Community theater and Community Chest. Intensely loyal and patriotic Americans, they are none the less inordinately proud of what Mark Twain called, "The loveliest fleet of islands that lies anchored in any ocean," and glad to share its delights.

HONOLULU'S
FIRST MULE-
DRAWN CAR

NOTES

NOTES

NOTES

NOTES

NOTES

NOTES